CW01213413

FRANCIS FRITH'S
ROCHDALE PHOTOGRAPHIC MEMORIES

THE FRANCIS FRITH COLLECTION

www.francisfrith.com

FRANCIS FRITH'S

ROCHDALE

PHOTOGRAPHIC MEMORIES

HANNAH HAYNES has a keen interest in photographic records. Collecting postcards of the Rochdale area is one of her hobbies, and she is Reference Librarian of the Rochdale Metropolitan Borough, having previously been Local Studies Librarian at both Middleton and Heywood. Her first book on Balderstone, Rochdale, was soon out of print, and two archive photograph histories of Middleton have gone to several reprints. Hannah also produced a successful history of Heywood. This is her first book for Francis Frith, and a long-awaited opportunity to look at the Rochdale area as a whole.

FRANCIS FRITH'S
PHOTOGRAPHIC MEMORIES

ROCHDALE

PHOTOGRAPHIC MEMORIES

HANNAH M HAYNES

First published in the United Kingdom in 2004 by
Frith Book Company Ltd

Limited Hardback Subscribers Edition Published in 2004
ISBN 1-85937-925-7

Paperback Edition 2004
ISBN 1-85937-846-3

Text and Design copyright © Frith Book Company Ltd
Photographs copyright © The Francis Frith Collection

The Frith photographs and the Frith logo are reproduced under licence from Heritage Photographic Resources Ltd, the owners of the Frith archive and trademarks

All rights reserved. No photograph in this publication may be sold to a third party other than in the original form of this publication, or framed for sale to a third party. No parts of this publication may be reproduced, stored in a retrieval system, or transmitted, in any form, or by any means, electronic, mechanical, photocopying, recording or otherwise, without the prior permission of the publishers and copyright holder.

British Library Cataloguing in Publication Data

Francis Frith's Rochdale - Photographic Memories
Hannah M Haynes

Frith Book Company Ltd
Frith's Barn, Teffont,
Salisbury, Wiltshire SP3 5QP
Tel: +44 (0) 1722 716 376
Email: info@francisfrith.co.uk
www.francisfrith.co.uk

Printed and bound in Great Britain

Front Cover: **ROCHDALE**, *Church Steps 1913* 65603t
Frontispiece: **ROCHDALE**, *Falinge Park 1913* 65605

The colour-tinting is for illustrative purposes only, and is not intended to be historically accurate

AS WITH ANY HISTORICAL DATABASE THE FRITH ARCHIVE IS CONSTANTLY BEING CORRECTED AND IMPROVED AND THE PUBLISHERS WOULD WELCOME INFORMATION ON OMISSIONS OR INACCURACIES

CONTENTS

FRANCIS FRITH: VICTORIAN PIONEER	7
ROCHDALE - AN INTRODUCTION	10
ROCHDALE	12
AROUND ROCHDALE	44
MIDDLETON AND HEYWOOD	62
WHITWORTH AND HEALEY DELL	76
INDEX	89
NAMES OF SUBSCRIBERS	90
Free Mounted Print Voucher	91

FRANCIS FRITH
VICTORIAN PIONEER

FRANCIS FRITH, founder of the world-famous photographic archive, was a complex and multi-talented man. A devout Quaker and a highly successful Victorian businessman, he was philosophical by nature and pioneering in outlook.

By 1855 he had already established a wholesale grocery business in Liverpool, and sold it for the astonishing sum of £200,000, which is the equivalent today of over £15,000,000. Now a very rich man, he was able to indulge his passion for travel. As a child he had pored over travel books written by early explorers, and his fancy and imagination had been stirred by family holidays to the sublime mountain regions of Wales and Scotland. 'What lands of spirit-stirring and enriching scenes and places!' he had written. He was to return to these scenes of grandeur in later years to 'recapture the thousands of vivid and tender memories', but with a different purpose. Now in his thirties, and captivated by the new science of photography, Frith set out on a series of pioneering journeys up the Nile and to the Near East that occupied him from 1856 until 1860.

INTRIGUE AND EXPLORATION

These far-flung journeys were packed with intrigue and adventure. In his life story, written when he was sixty-three, Frith tells of being held captive by bandits, and of fighting 'an awful midnight battle to the very point of surrender with a deadly pack of hungry, wild dogs'. Wearing flowing Arab costume, Frith arrived at Akaba by camel sixty years before Lawrence of Arabia, where he encountered 'desert princes and rival sheikhs, blazing with jewel-hilted swords'.

He was the first photographer to venture beyond the sixth cataract of the Nile. Africa was still the mysterious 'Dark Continent', and Stanley and Livingstone's historic meeting was a decade into the future. The conditions for picture taking confound belief. He laboured for hours in his wicker dark-room in the sweltering heat of the desert, while the volatile chemicals fizzed dangerously in their trays. Back in London he exhibited his photographs and was 'rapturously cheered' by members of the Royal Society. His reputation as a photographer was made overnight.

VENTURE OF A LIFE-TIME

Characteristically, Frith quickly spotted the opportunity to create a new business as a specialist publisher of photographs. He lived in an era of immense and sometimes violent change.

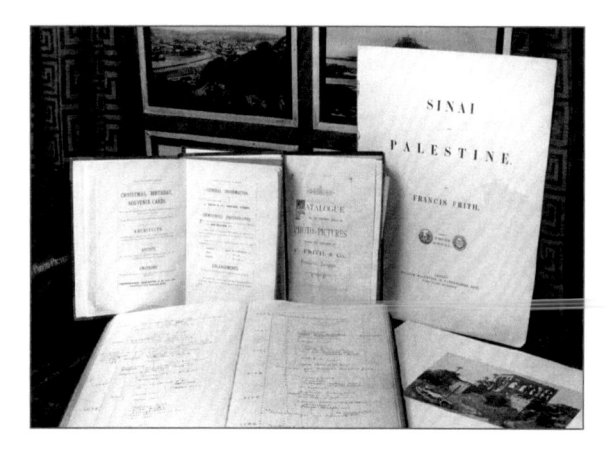

For the poor in the early part of Victoria's reign work was exhausting and the hours long, and people had precious little free time to enjoy themselves. Most had no transport other than a cart or gig at their disposal, and rarely travelled far beyond the boundaries of their own town or village. However, by the 1870s the railways had threaded their way across the country, and Bank Holidays and half-day Saturdays had been made obligatory by Act of Parliament. All of a sudden the working man and his family were able to enjoy days out and see a little more of the world.

With typical business acumen, Francis Frith foresaw that these new tourists would enjoy having souvenirs to commemorate their days out. In 1860 he married Mary Ann Rosling and set out on a new career: his aim was to photograph every city, town and village in Britain. For the next thirty years he travelled the country by train and by pony and trap, producing fine photographs of seaside resorts and beauty spots that were keenly bought by millions of Victorians. These prints were painstakingly pasted into family albums and pored over during the dark nights of winter, rekindling precious memories of summer excursions.

THE RISE OF FRITH & CO

Frith's studio was soon supplying retail shops all over the country. To meet the demand he gathered about him a small team of photographers, and published the work of independent artist-photographers of the calibre of Roger Fenton and Francis Bedford. In order to gain some understanding of the scale of Frith's business one only has to look at the catalogue issued by Frith & Co in 1886: it runs to some 670 pages, listing not only many thousands of views of the British Isles but also many photographs of most European countries, and China, Japan, the USA and Canada - note the sample page shown on page 9 from the hand-written Frith & Co ledgers recording the pictures. By 1890 Frith had created the greatest specialist photographic publishing company in the world, with over 2,000 sales outlets - more than the combined number that Boots and WH Smith have today! The picture on the next page shows the Frith & Co display board at Ingleton in the Yorkshire Dales (left of window). Beautifully constructed with a mahogany frame and gilt inserts, it could display up to a dozen local scenes.

POSTCARD BONANZA

The ever-popular holiday postcard we know today took many years to develop. In 1870 the Post Office issued the first plain cards, with a pre-printed stamp on one face. In 1894 they allowed other publishers' cards to be sent through the mail with an attached adhesive halfpenny stamp. Demand grew rapidly, and in 1895 a new size of postcard was permitted called the court card, but there was little room for illustration. In 1899, a year after Frith's death, a new card measuring 5.5 x 3.5 inches became the standard format, but it was not until 1902 that the divided back came into being, so that the address and message could be on one face and a full-size illustration on the other. Frith & Co were in the vanguard of postcard development: Frith's sons Eustace and Cyril continued their father's monumental task, expanding the number of views offered to the public and recording more and more places in Britain, as the coasts and countryside were opened up to mass travel.

Francis Frith had died in 1898 at his villa in Cannes, his great project still growing. The archive he created continued in business for another seventy years. By 1970 it contained over a third of a million pictures showing 7,000 British towns and villages.

FRANCIS FRITH'S LEGACY

Frith's legacy to us today is of immense significance and value, for the magnificent archive of evocative photographs he created provides a unique record of change in the cities, towns and villages throughout Britain over a century and more. Frith and his fellow studio photographers revisited locations many times down the years to update their views, compiling for us an enthralling and colourful pageant of British life and character.

We are fortunate that Frith was dedicated to recording the minutiae of everyday life. For it is this sheer wealth of visual data, the painstaking chronicle of changes in dress, transport, street layouts, buildings, housing, engineering and landscape that captivates us so much today. His remarkable images offer us a powerful link with the past and with the lives of our ancestors.

THE VALUE OF THE ARCHIVE TODAY

Computers have now made it possible for Frith's many thousands of images to be accessed almost instantly. Frith's images are increasingly used as visual resources, by social historians, by researchers into genealogy and ancestry, by architects and town planners, and by teachers involved in local history projects.

In addition, the archive offers every one of us an opportunity to examine the places where we and our families have lived and worked down the years. Highly successful in Frith's own era, the archive is now, a century and more on, entering a new phase of popularity. Historians consider the Francis Frith Collection to be of prime national importance. It is the only archive of its kind remaining in private ownership. Francis Frith's archive is now housed in an historic timber barn in the beautiful village of Teffont in Wiltshire. Its founder would not recognize the archive office as it is today. In place of the many thousands of dusty boxes containing glass plate negatives and an all-pervading odour of photographic chemicals, there are now ranks of computer screens. He would be amazed to watch his images travelling round the world at unimaginable speeds through internet lines.

The archive's future is both bright and exciting. Francis Frith, with his unshakeable belief in making photographs available to the greatest number of people, would undoubtedly approve of what is being done today with his lifetime's work. His photographs depicting our shared past are now bringing pleasure and enlightenment to millions around the world a century and more after his death.

ROCHDALE
AN INTRODUCTION

ROCHDALE IS ONE of very few modern-day industrial towns to be mentioned in the Domesday Book of 1086. A market charter was granted in 1251 and in 1586 Rochdale was described as a well-frequented market town. It prospered largely through its handloom weaving, which was usually linked with local farming. The Annals of Rochdale record a large number of sheep on its moors in 1800 at the peak of the handloom weaving era; the Annals also record that 8,000 pieces of flannel were produced in 1825. The woollen-weaving hamlets were largely self-contained with their halls, folds, corn mills and coalmines clustered around the brooks and Rochdale has mainly developed around them - many weavers' cottages still remain. Many of the merchants employing the handloom weavers went on to build their own steam-powered textile mills, Henry Kelsall and James Royds being among them.

Rochdale became a parliamentary borough in 1832 and gained a municipal charter in 1856, with the powers and property of the old Commissioners conferred to the Corporation in 1858. Many of the photograph captions tell of the selfless service and generosity of prominent Rochdale councillors. Middleton and Heywood, important towns in their own right, became part of the Metropolitan Borough of Rochdale in 1974. Rochdale's woollen trade had close links with Halifax, initially by packhorse routes, followed by turnpike roads, canal and railway, and it remained loyal to wool; but cotton manufacture increased in Rochdale over the years. Middleton was well known for its silk weaving and Heywood was almost entirely a product of the cotton trade.

During the Industrial Revolution, the river Roach and its tributaries provided water power for textile mills. The town's population increased fourfold during the 19th century, as people from rural areas moved in seeking work. Dwellings, shops and warehouses sprang up in Rochdale town centre on either side of the river. There were corn, dyeing and fulling mills, and also a forge; all these were near what later became the Wellington Hotel. Since 1630 there had been a hump-backed bridge to the west of the ford at the bottom of Church Lane. The Roach ran open until the 20th century, when it was covered in four stages. The first stretch to be covered was Wellington Bridge to Yorkshire Street, which was finished in July 1904; the second Yorkshire Street to Newgate, July 1910; the third Newgate to Theatre Street, June 1923; and lastly Wellington Bridge to Weir Street, 30 January 1926.

Rochdale was the most extensive parish in the Salford Hundred and an important ecclesiastical centre. The earliest markets were held near the church, where parades and celebrations were also held. The main road from east to west passed in front of the church, having come via what is now Milnrow Road, through School Lane (named after the Grammar School), continuing across Broadfield, down Dane Street and on to the ford at Oakenrod Weir. The main route from south to north crossed this road as it went into Church Lane, the old roads from Manchester and Oldham having joined just south of the church. Rochdale was a Non-conformist stronghold and church and chapel have had a major influence on the town.

The photographs portray a town emerging from the Victorian era with a strong sense of identity, proudly expressed in its magnificent Town Hall. They were taken after the period of rapid expansion and many reflect the Victorians' fondness for monuments and statues and their appreciation of pleasure grounds such as public parks, lakes and natural woodland. The Victorians saw parks as places where those who had moved into Rochdale from more rural areas could recapture their youth and escape ill-ventilated cottages; the sick could recover, and children could play safely.

It is interesting to note that many of the photographs are of features now attracting heritage lottery funding for restoration, as they appear to have been created with posterity in mind! The photographs also have a wider brief. They show local industry, for example: textile mills appear almost as an intrusion on some early Rochdale town centre scenes, but in the Whitworth Valley they are centre stage. Also, the vivid images of traffic congestion in Rochdale town centre in the 1960s are already part of Rochdale's history.

A whole section of this book is devoted to Middleton and Heywood. Snapshots of other industrial areas, such as Castleton, Shaw and Whitworth, also give a wider dimension to the book. There are glimpses of Healey Dell, parts of which appear to be little changed since Anglo Saxon times, contrasting with the more modern man-made tourist attraction of Hollingworth Lake.

John Bright, the orator and radical MP and a passionate agitator for the repeal of the Corn Laws, has pride of place as Rochdale's most famous citizen. A statue in his honour (now in Broadfield Park) with its bidding 'Be just and fear not' was erected on 24 October 1891 by public subscription in the Town Hall Square. It was one of several in England; others were unveiled in Birmingham on 11 April 1881, in Albert Square, Manchester on 10 October 1891, and at Westminster Hall on 11 February 1896, symbolic, perhaps, of the influence of Rochdalians nationwide.

Rochdale is justly proud of its town centre with its magnificent Town Hall, which was opened in 1871. The building of the Town Hall, the Esplanade and the formation of Broadfield Park, all in a relatively short time, brought a new structure to the town centre. Before this, development had been more informal. There was a ford across the Roach at the bottom of Church Lane where the old road from the south crossed the river. The river has changed its course over the centuries, and used to be wider. It was diverted for the construction of a bridge for the Rochdale and Manchester Turnpike Trust Road (which became Manchester Road), having previously flowed to the north rather than to the south of the Holme. The covering of the Roach in various stages changed the appearance of the Town Centre dramatically, producing an air of spaciousness. The Esplanade was laid out in 1868, during the construction of the Town Hall; it received its name in 1872, at the suggestion of Alderman Taylor, who overturned the Corporation's proposal to name it Corporation Street.

FRANCIS FRITH'S - ROCHDALE

ROCHDALE

CHURCH STEPS *1913* 65603

This is probably Frith's best loved photograph of Rochdale – it appeared on an early postcard. The 122 steps lead down from the parish church to the town centre 80ft below. The churchwardens' accounts for 1660 record that 24 shillings was paid for 8 loads of 'great stone' from Blackstone Edge for the steps. Taylors House on the right was occupied by Worth & Worth, solicitors, for many years. When it was demolished in 1934 it contained a huge stone water tank, the town's first reservoir, constructed by the Taylors in 1760. The water was drawn from Packer Spout.

ROCHDALE

THE PARISH CHURCH AND PACKER SPOUT GARDENS *c1965*
R42022

The church steps are on the left. Buildings on Leyland Brow, to the right of the steps, and the corn mill below were demolished in 1934. The Ecclesiastical Commissioners had given land between the church and the Town Hall to the town and the area was landscaped, with steps in the centre leading up to Packer Spout, the spring referred to in the caption to 65603 (page 12).

THE PARISH CHURCH *1892* 30399

The records of the parish church of St Chad date back to 1194, although evidence of a Saxon wall points to an earlier building. Parts of the present building date back to the 13th century. Among many alterations, the tower was heightened and its clock removed in 1873, W H Crossland, designer of the Town Hall, being the architect at the time.

FRANCIS FRITH'S - ROCHDALE

◀ **BROADFIELD PARK**
1892 30402

The Corporation rented this glebe land from the Ecclesiastical Commissioners in 1868 to develop as Rochdale's first park (the ground rent was remitted for all time in 1894). A provision market was held near the church until the mid 16th century, when it moved to the Market Place, but cattle fairs remained at Church Stile until the cattle fair ground in Theatre Street was opened in 1877. Broadfield was also used for parades and celebrations and as grazing for the vicar's horse and cows. The park opened in 1874; opponents said that plants would not flourish so close to the town centre, but they were proved wrong.

14

◄ THE PARISH CHURCH
The Interior
1892 30400

A west gallery was added in 1693 and a gallery on the south side in 1698, but both were removed in 1855. The north aisle was rebuilt in 1856 and a clerestory was added. The pews were replaced by chairs in 1952.

◄ BROADFIELD PARK
1895 36766

Councillor Edward Taylor and Alderman George Leach Ashworth, who was twice mayor of Rochdale, were largely responsible for acquiring the 16 acres that form the park. Ashworth's statue was unveiled on 1 June 1878 - it cost 800 guineas. The inscription states that he was 'a devoted friend of the public'.
The bandstand, given by Alderman J Duckworth MP, was opened on 4 November 1893.

FRANCIS FRITH'S - ROCHDALE

THE ENTRANCE TO BROADFIELD PARK
c1955 R42002

We have entered from opposite the vicarage gates. The spire of St Alban's Church, demolished in 1973, is just visible to the right of the Ashworth statue (left). The park's first bowling green was opened on 1 July 1908 and the second in 1927. A £2 million redevelopment plan for the park, mainly funded by heritage lottery money, was announced in July 2003, and a warden is being appointed.

THE ESPLANADE *1892* 30398
Looking towards the town centre from Manchester Road. The magnificent Town Hall comes into view beyond Broadfield Park slopes, created from 1870 onwards. Willow Grove, a private dwelling, is on the left, with the library, built in 1884, to its right. It was still safe to walk in the centre of the road with a horse and cart (centre)!

THE FOUNTAIN *1902* 48577

Officially described as a 'drinking fountain for horses, cattle and dogs', it became known as the Angel, owing to the 15ft-high white Sicilian marble statue on a Yorkshire stone base. Ellen McKinnon gave it to the town in memory of her mother, a sister of John Entwisle of Foxholes. The troughs were removed just before the Second World War for road alterations. The Angel remained until April 1961, when the official reason for its removal to the Princess Street Corporation Works Yard was its rapid deterioration due to erosion. It subsequently fell to pieces, as repair was thought too expensive.

FRANCIS FRITH'S - ROCHDALE

ROCHDALE

THE ESPLANADE
1902 48575

The Angel graced the town centre approach from 1899. Another elegant new feature was the Dialect Writers' Memorial, erected on the Park Slopes in 1900. The youths round the Angel, happy at the novelty of posing for a photograph, were soon to appear on one of Rochdale's first postcards.

FRANCIS FRITH'S - ROCHDALE

◀ **THE ESPLANADE**
1913 65600

An electric tram to Sudden crosses the tram track to Bury. The Art Gallery and Museum, opened 3 April 1903, had an extension added on the left in 1912, with its sculptured stone panels depicting science, art and literature. Following heritage lottery and Council funding the complex of buildings has been restored and adapted to house the Touchstones Arts and Heritage Centre.

ROCHDALE

◀ **THE VIEW FROM THE PARK SLOPES** *1913* 65604

Mills crowd in towards the town centre, following the course of the river Roach and its tributary the Spodden. Textile mills reached their peak of prosperity at this time. Their pollution has blackened the Yorkshire stone of the Library, Museum and Art Gallery, varying according to the order in which they were built! Trinity Presbyterian Church, opened in 1869, is even darker. It was a familiar landmark until the early 1980s, when the disused building was demolished following a fire. St Chad's School on the left became the Gymnasium in 1897, and the Nurses' Home is to its right.

◀ **THE MEMORIAL** *1902* 48576

The Dialect Writers' Memorial, erected in 1900, was sometimes referred to as the Poets' Memorial. It honours Edwin Waugh, Oliver Ormerod, John Trafford Clegg and Margaret Rebecca Lahee, but Tim Bobbin is a notable omission. In 1986 the name of Rochdale's much-loved Harvey Kershaw MBE was added. The mills near the Roach at the eastern end of the town centre are on the left.

FRANCIS FRITH'S - ROCHDALE

ROCHDALE

THE TOWN HALL
1892 30397

Plans were requested for a Town Hall costing about £20,000, but by its opening on 27 September 1871 the bill was £160,000.
W H Crossland designed the 88ft-long building. Its spire rose to 240ft, but was destroyed by fire on 10 April 1883. During Queen Victoria's Golden Jubilee of 1887 it was replaced by a 190ft spire designed by Alfred Waterhouse, the architect of Manchester Town Hall. The 12 bells and a carillon of 14 tunes (ranging from 'Easter Hymn' to 'Home Sweet Home') of the original spire were reduced to 5 bells and no tunes in the new spire.

FRANCIS FRITH'S - ROCHDALE

▼ **THE GRAMMAR SCHOOL** *1895* 36765

Opened in 1847, this was Rochdale Grammar School's second building. Dr Matthew Parker, Archbishop of Canterbury, founded the school in 1565. He was a meticulous man who never missed anything and the nickname 'nosey parker' is derived from him. The local historian Dr Henry Brierley described the school as having one fire, a leaking roof and appalling sanitation, although it was a fine-looking building when new.

◀ **THE NURSES' HOME** *1906* 54131

The Queen Victoria Memorial Nurses' Home opened in 1904 on the former site of the second Grammar School. The Accrington brick building has a statue of Victoria above its door. The Gymnasium, formerly St Chad's School, was next door until the 1940s, when it was demolished for an extension to the Home. Marydon Hotels Limited converted the Home into the Broadfield Hotel in 1973.

THE MANOR HOUSE *1898* 41026

Rochdale adopted this red brick building, correctly named the Orchard, as the Manor House because it was the residence of the Deardens before they purchased the manor from the poet Lord Byron. Described as new in 1702, it had an orchard, a sundial, a lake and extensive gardens. It was demolished in 1922 and the war memorial was built on its site.

FRANCIS FRITH'S - ROCHDALE

THE WAR MEMORIAL *c1965* R42030

Alderman Cunliffe OBE JP purchased the Manor House estate and gave it to the Corporation, but the Great War interrupted plans for development. It was eventually used for the site of the war memorial, which was designed by Sir Edwin Lutyens, architect of the Whitehall cenotaph. It was a popular choice and around 50,000 people attended the unveiling on 26 November 1922.

ROCHDALE

THE WAR MEMORIAL AND THE POST OFFICE *c1965* R42031

A tribute to those who fell in the Second World War was added to the cenotaph. The Ministry of Works built the post office of Portland Stone in 1927 in a restrained Baroque style. The Beva Group have recently spent £250,000 on the building and plan to spend more.

THE MEMORIAL GARDENS *c1965* R42021

In 1947 land behind the war memorial was landscaped as sunken gardens and their 1.3 acres became the new Gardens of Remembrance. The Hippodrome on the left was where Gracie Fields, one of Rochdale's most famous citizens, began her singing career: she came joint first in a talent show at the age of 10 and won 10s 6d.

FRANCIS FRITH'S · ROCHDALE

ROCHDALE

THE ENTRANCE TO YORKSHIRE STREET
1898 41023

Work started on the Oldham Joint Stock Bank (now the HSBC), on the right, in 1892, and it was officially opened on 30 September 1895. The Lancashire and Yorkshire Bank (now Barclays, left) opened on 4 July 1896. Both are faced with Yorkshire stone, which became blackened but later cleaned well.

FRANCIS FRITH'S - ROCHDALE

TOWN HALL SQUARE
1913 65599

The Roach was covered here in 1910. The Oldham Joint Stock Bank on the right had become the London City and Midland Bank. On the left the new building is inscribed Rochdale Vintners Co Ltd 1911 and it extends through to Yorkshire Street as Yates' Wine Lodge. It has listed building status. The men with the bike in front of it are wearing boaters.

TOWN HALL SQUARE *1892* 30396

The statue of John Bright MP stands in front of Charles Kershaw's Central Corn Mill. The statue cost £2,000 and was unveiled on 24 October 1891; it stood close to the Town Hall, whose foundation stone Bright had laid 25 years earlier. He was born at Greenbank, near his father's mill, on 16 November 1811 and he died at One Ash on 27 March 1889.

JOHN BRIGHT'S STATUE *1898* 41022

The bronze statue depicts Bright as the born orator; he has been called 'Rochdale's greatest townsman'. A famous quotation below reads: 'My clients have not been generally the rich and the great, but rather the poor and the lowly. They cannot give me place and dignity and wealth but honourable service in their cause yielding that which is of higher and more lasting value'. Entering Parliament in 1843, he became a leader of the Anti-Corn Law League, Member of the Privy Council and President of the Board of Trade. Public uproar followed the removal of his statue to Broadfield Park in June 1923.

ONE ASH
1898 41025

John Bright's father Jacob built a cotton mill at Greenbank in 1809 and John became a partner when he was aged 16. John built his home, One Ash, opposite the mill in 1839. He spotted a young ash tree growing by a fence and named the house after it. The tree thrived and One Ash remains today, but its gardens no longer extend as far as Cronkeyshaw Common.

THE FRIENDS' MEETING HOUSE *1898* 41027

Jacob Bright was a leading member of the Society of Friends in Rochdale who built this Meeting House in George Street in 1808, when Quaker merchants and their families numbered around 100. John Bright worshipped here too and was buried with his family in the graveyard. By 1968 the building had become too expensive for the Friends to maintain. Their offer to convey it to the Corporation was declined and it was demolished.

ROCHDALE

▲ **BROADWAY** *1906* 54124

The Roach was covered here in 1904 and the shelter appears to be the one that formerly overhung the river. It was soon to be replaced. The Manor House can be seen to the right. The centre of the town is starting to look spacious and elegant.

◀ *detail of 54124*

FRANCIS FRITH'S - ROCHDALE

▼ **BROADWAY** *1906* 54122

An open-topped electric tram has just arrived from Sudden. Steam trams used a narrow gauge track and electric trams could not enter the town centre until after May 1903, when authorisation was given to convert to standard gauge. Meanwhile, trams to Bury started at Dane Street. By 1905 electric trams had completely superseded the steam trams, which started in 1882.

▶ **BROADWAY**
1906 54125

Butts Mill, a woollen mill (left), opened in 1835. To its right are Bowling Green Mill (a cotton mill) and Duncan Street Mill (another woollen mill). They were owned by Kelsall & Kemp. Before 1835, Henry Kelsall had his wool woven by domestic workers and sold his finished cloth at the local market. The area known as the Butts covered a wide area and was named after its former use as an archery ground. It was also used as a village green and assembly ground; here maypole dances and parades were held, and here orators such as John Bright spoke. The Butts extended from the Walk to Butts Mill.

ROCHDALE

◀ **BROADWAY**
c1910 30397a

In 1907 plans were approved for this combined tram shelter, toilets and office, said to be one of the best in the British Isles. It remained until 1933 – the trams had stopped running in the previous year. Flat caps were still popular, but some of the men are again wearing boaters. To the right of the Walk an elegantly dressed woman contrasts with one in clogs and shawl (see 30397b below).

▶ **BROADWAY**
The Walk
c1910 30397b

This was described as an ancient common way in 1702, when it led to Lower Yates, New House and orchards or walks. Walter Vavasour built the block of buildings forming the Walk in the early 1800s, partly on the site of the yard of Eagle Inn. The Vavasours, who were woollen merchants and built Butts House, also built the former iron footbridge leading to the Walk in 1824.

FRANCIS FRITH'S - ROCHDALE

ROCHDALE

THE TOWN CENTRE
c1955 R42005

Lea Scott, an optician's, is on the left and Haworth's next door still has both men's and ladies' wear departments at this time. The bank in the centre had become Martin's, with the building still largely the same as when it was built. Burton's the tailor's (right) had added an ornate exterior to the former modest buildings to the right of the Walk.

FRANCIS FRITH'S - ROCHDALE

▶ **THE TOWN CENTRE**
c1955 R42006

A number 9 bus from Ashton has just arrived on the left. Buses and their shelters have become an important feature of the centre; other traffic is still relatively light. F Holt's shoe shop can be seen on the left of the Walk.

ROCHDALE

◀ **THE TOWN CENTRE**
c1965 R42032

It is only ten years after photograph R42006 but traffic has increased dramatically, with buses everywhere. Their termini remained in the centre until the Bus Station was opened on 16 May 1978. A mill still survives close to the centre: Hardman's, whose top is just visible behind the ABC Cinema (centre).

FRANCIS FRITH'S - ROCHDALE

▶ **THE TOWN CENTRE** *c1965* R42023

Martin's Bank (centre left), on the left of Yorkshire Street, has lost its turret and other roof top features during modernisation and the Midland Bank has been cleaned. Buses are again very prominent.

▼ **NEWGATE** *c1910* 30400a

In 1907 the Corporation cut a new thoroughfare across Newgate, demolishing the Circus and the old Hippodrome and linking Blackwater Street with the Esplanade. The Red Lion Inn got a new facade on its western side, prolonging its life until a Compulsory Purchase Order forced its demolition in 1973, ready for the new shopping centre and market. The Red Lion dated back to at least 1792, when it was called Blackwater. It originally faced onto the lower part of Blackwater Street, which later became Lord Street. The new Hippodrome on the right opened on 16 November 1908 and was demolished in 1970.

ROCHDALE

◀ **DRAKE STREET**
1906 54126

Drake Street was cut through swampy land between two small hills in 1810 when Dr Drake, vicar of Rochdale, started leasing and selling part of the vicarage estate. Church Lane was previously the old route down to the centre. The restaurant and dining rooms of James Duckworth's Temperance and Commercial Hotel, opened in 1886, are on the right. They were also known as the Reform Club Buildings, because the club, of which James Duckworth was a prominent member, met here. Duckworth's bread and confectionery department was also here. The Co-op purchased the premises for their Fashion Corner in 1922.

41

FRANCIS FRITH'S - ROCHDALE

▲**YORKSHIRE STREET** *1892* 30401

Originally High Street, its approach from the ford across the Roach was via Bull Brow. This old route to Yorkshire was widened in 1897 when the building on the left was demolished. The shops on the right are Thompson Bros, clothiers, at number 16, followed by Wild's Hat Manufactory, established in 1850, then Freeman, Hardy & Willis (boots and shoes) at number 20, Thomas Davies, grocer, and J & J Thomas & Son, chemists, at number 24 by Butts Avenue. S E Wild, a hosier and shirt maker, occupied number 28, later owned by Senior's. The jeweller's shop with the clock is A Williamson's.

ROCHDALE

▲ **DRAKE STREET** *c1960* R42012

The buildings have not changed much, but the street has lost its hustle and bustle. Car parking was allowed at this time. The Rochdale Observer office on the left still had its old clock, which has since been replaced.

▲ **THE TECHNICAL SCHOOL** *1895* 36764

This Accrington brick school was opened on 26 April 1893 and among its impressive facilities was a huge weaving room. Land opposite often saw overspills of crowds from town centre events such as the unveiling of the war memorial until it was developed as St Chad's Gardens in 1925. The Technical School ended its days as Broadfield Upper School and it was demolished in 1988.

FRANCIS FRITH'S - ROCHDALE

AROUND ROCHDALE

Hollingworth Lake is Rochdale's oldest major tourist attraction. It was especially popular in the days before cheap rail tickets to the seaside became available. The 104 acres of the lake are only 3 miles from Rochdale centre and were a popular rendezvous by the mid 1860s. Healey Dell has been an attraction of a different type for much longer, probably since Anglo-Saxon times. In 1905 the Edwardian Falinge Park was opened north of Rochdale centre. Something of its original beauty can be seen in this chapter. Castleton developed largely because of its proximity to the canal and railway, making it suitable for mill building. Its railway station was opened on 4 June 1839 in the hamlet then known as Bluepits, and the station's name was changed to Castleton in 1875. Tweedale & Smalley's vast Castleton complex for textile machinery manufacture was completed by 1894 and they employed over 1,000 workers at their peak. Whipp & Bourne started business in 1903. The Ensor, Arrow and Crest cotton mills were built next to the canal around 1907. Shaw had to wait until 1863 for its railway, but the industrial expansion that followed was also substantial; the photographs capture a character that is uniquely Shaw's.

HOLLINGWORTH LAKE *1892* 30401a
Formed as a feeder for Rochdale Canal in 1800, the lake became known as 'the Weavers' Seaport', popular with people from Manchester, Bradford, Bury and Oldham for a day trip - it also boasted enough attractions for two days! Easter was a busy time. Many came by the Lancashire & Yorkshire Railway, initially alighting at Littleborough Station, which opened on 3 July 1839, with the option of getting off at Smithy Bridge from 1868.

AROUND ROCHDALE

HOLLINGWORTH LAKE
1895 36777

This is the southern or 't'Cheshire side' of the lake, with the roof of the Lancashire & Yorkshire Hotel, which opened on 17 December 1875, just visible in the centre. It had stabling, a landing stage, a ticket office, a dancing platform and a band often in attendance. It closed in December 1911.

LITTLEBOROUGH, *Lake Bank c1950* L182001
The Fisherman's Inn (the white building on the right) is the lake's oldest inn. It has outlived the pleasure grounds 'brilliantly illuminated by gas', the photographic studios producing miniatures for lockets and brooches, the wedding breakfasts, and the steam roundabout with horses which were totally natural-looking and undecorated.

FRANCIS FRITH'S - ROCHDALE

◀ **LITTLEBOROUGH**
The Lake Hotel Cafe c1950
L182004

The cafe was in the former Rowing Club building of 1860. It had a spacious balcony with good views, two billiard tables on the upper floor, gas lighting and two clocks to avoid missing the ferries. The ferries were timed to link in with passing trains. The Lake Hotel had opened in 1872 with a floating landing stage, a subaqueous telegraph linking it to the booking office for ferry steamers, a skating rink, a bowling green and well laid-out gardens with a brass band often in attendance.

AROUND ROCHDALE

◀ **LITTLEBOROUGH**
The Fisherman's Inn c1950 L182003

The inn dates back to 1845 and was formed out of a group of farm buildings. Its first victualler also farmed 12 acres. There was good stabling and a lock-up coach house. A four-wheel dray backed into the lake here in 1869, falling into 14ft of water; two people drowned.

◀ **LITTLEBOROUGH**
Lake Bank c1950
L182002

This shop at the corner of Smithy Bridge Road was formerly Nichol's Teashop. It was still serving teas at this time, or you could just sit on a bench outside and enjoy the fresh air and an ice cream. The slating of gable end walls (we can see examples further along Lake Bank) was commonplace in Rochdale as a protection against severe weather conditions on exposed walls.

FRANCIS FRITH'S - ROCHDALE

AROUND ROCHDALE

LITTLEBOROUGH
Hollingworth Lake
c1960 L182010

The temperature is rising and on a hot day in the early 1960s it seems as if all of Rochdale has headed for the lake. The paddleboats were popular, whilst some were content to settle for a swim or dip their feet in the water before queuing at the ice cream vans. Today, the Visitor Centre attracts around 130,000 people each year.

▶ LITTLEBOROUGH
The Harbour, Hollingworth Lake
1955 L182006

The lake has attracted racing skiffs, ferry steamers and fishing punts in its time. The boathouse on the north side has also been the base for rowing clubs. Fishing was 6d a day or 10s a season in 1872. A record-breaking 26lbs 14oz pike was caught in 1982. In 1980 the lake became one of the top ten country parks in the country.

◀ FALINGE PARK
1906 56467

Mount Falinge was built by James Royds around 1800. The family were woollen merchants, who employed weavers working in their own cottages such as Bentmeadows. Alderman Sir Samuel Turner purchased Mount Falinge with 18 acres of grounds for the town in 1902 to mark Edward VII's coronation. The final cost to him was £14,000. Mount Falinge was damaged by fire in 1975 and only the facade and terrace remain.

AROUND ROCHDALE

▲ **FALINGE PARK** *1906* 56468

Samuel Turner spent £2,300 on laying out and planting the grounds of Mount Falinge as a public park, which opened on 5 August 1905 amid great celebrations. On 22 June 1911 he gave an extra 4.5 acres to commemorate the coronation of George V. This is Fountain Court; the fountain remains today, but it is filled with plants.

◀ **FALINGE PARK** *1906* 56470

Like Broadfield Park, the grounds were developed as a mixture of formal and informal areas with breathtaking lawns and a lake. To people living in cramped terraced houses with small back yards, these parks offered a breath of fresh air and the prospect of relaxation with the family.

FRANCIS FRITH'S - ROCHDALE

▼ **FALINGE PARK** *1913* 65605

The sheltered Floral Court (or Sun Gardens) have always been a popular sitting area with their well maintained flower beds. They are still beautiful today, and the park is well tended, but the Council has reluctantly closed the hothouses and outbuildings due to vandalism.

▶ **ST JOHN'S ROMAN CATHOLIC CHURCH** *c1960* R42003

Erected in 1924, this church replaced a building of 1829. It is built of red brick and York stone, surmounted by a large concrete dome once covered with copper and crowned by the four short and narrow arms of a Greek cross. Standing opposite the railway station, it creates a good first impression of the town to visitors, and has recently been restored.

AROUND ROCHDALE

◀ **CASTLETON**
Manchester Road
1951 C758007

The road on the right was formerly John Street. It became Queensway in 1927, when it first cut across to Oldham Road, Lower Place. After Kingsway was built in 1935 it linked up with Queensway, forming a by-pass that relieved the centre of Rochdale of traffic going from Manchester to Yorkshire.

▶ **CASTLETON**
St Martin's Parish Church
1951 C758005

Bishop Fraser alighted at Bluepits station on 14 June 1862 to consecrate the church, which is built of Yorkshire stone. Mr R Stott of Trub Cotton Mill gave a clock for the tower in 1868. In 1874 the bell from Castleton Print Works, Trows, was presented to the church. The church has recently been restored and re-ordered with heritage lottery funding, making it more versatile for worship and community use. In its elevated position it is a local landmark and visible from the M62.

FRANCIS FRITH'S - ROCHDALE

AROUND ROCHDALE

CASTLETON
The George and Dragon Hotel 1951
C758002

Designed by Edgar Wood, the inn opened on 18 February 1897; the licence had been transferred from the previous inn at Trub Farmhouse. The mock-Tudor front was added later. Original carved dragons have survived on either side of the painted sign of St George on horseback killing the dragon. Posters on the right are for the municipal elections of 10 May 1951. One urges onlookers: 'Your choice Arthur Tweedale again for Castleton'.

FRANCIS FRITH'S - ROCHDALE

▲ **CASTLETON,** *The Congregational Church 1951* C758006

The foundation stone was laid here on 15 May 1869, when it was anticipated that Heywood Road would go through to Heywood, but a large bog prevented this and the church remained on a quiet road. Even so, extra classrooms were built in 1889. The corrugated iron building was purchased in 1959 to house the Sunday School, but it was later moved by the Scouts and Cubs to use as their HQ. The church became Castleton United Reformed Church, and the listed building is currently up for sale (summer 2004). The remaining 15 to 20 members hope to join Castleton Moor Methodists.

◀ **CASTLETON**
St Gabriel's Old School, Church and Hall 1951 C758004

Erected on the lower slopes of Foxhill, Castleton in 1885, these buildings replaced a former church. Another new church on Milne Street was opened on 30 August 1953, but the school remained on the hill. St Martin's Church can be seen on the left.

WALSDEN, *The Church and the Lock c1960* W219003

The Rochdale Canal was built as a cheaper alternative to turnpike roads for Rochdale's woollen trade. Reaching Littleborough from Sowerby Bridge in 1788, it was completed through to Manchester by 1804. An Act of 1952 closed the waterway to traffic along most of its length. A £23.8 million investment enabled Rochdale to link up with the national canal network again in 2002.

FRANCIS FRITH'S - ROCHDALE

AROUND ROCHDALE

▲ **WALSDEN** *c1960* W219002

Rochdale became an important textile manufacturing town, but its close proximity to the Pennines has meant that beautiful countryside has always been within half an hour's travel. Walsden had its own mills.

◄ **SHAW,** *Market Street c1950* S747007

Shaw developed as part of Crompton and by the early 1900s it had 29 spinning mills. The Lancashire & Yorkshire Railway brought cheap coal for the textile trade from 1863, passing Shaw's own Jubilee Colliery. Most local needs could be found on Market Street, with its stone-fronted shops. Many of Shaw's sturdy stone terraced houses had no bathrooms, and a tin bath is on sale on the left. Shop signs have been made with pride. The triangular-topped frontage right of centre is James Duckworth's grocer's shop. Shaw became part of Oldham in 1974.

FRANCIS FRITH'S - ROCHDALE

AROUND ROCHDALE

SHAW
Chamber Road c1950
S747006

The stone-fronted houses match the shops with their sturdiness and 'built to last' qualities. Slightly superior to many factory houses, with their small gardens, the terrace on the right has a dated stone on the second house: 'Built in the year of AD 1897 Victoria's Reign'. Its first house, Green Bank, is bigger than the rest and has a bay window, being built for a mill manager or the owner of the row. Stone sett paths and some flagstone walls dividing the back yards still remain today behind the stone terraces to both left and right.

FRANCIS FRITH'S - ROCHDALE

MIDDLETON AND HEYWOOD

Middleton and Heywood have been part of the Rochdale Metropolitan Borough since 1974. Middleton is thought to date back to Saxon times. It retained a traditional structure of hall, fold, park and corn mill in close proximity to St Leonard's Church until Middleton Hall was demolished in 1845. Once the Hall had gone, Middleton lacked an obvious centre, although the Market Place became a hive of activity. Unlike Rochdale, it did not opt to build an impressive town hall, abandoning plans to demolish the Boar's Head in 1888 and build one on its site. The building of the Arndale Centre in 1972 brought major change to its shopping centre. The photographs here are a glimpse of assets that Middleton valued; but the Market Place and Central Gardens have since been lost, sad to say. Much of Heywood was formerly in the Heap Township of Bury. It was the building of the cathedral-like St Luke's Church in 1862 that established a focal point for the town. In 1867 Heywood was extended to include land within a radius of one mile of the church. The Local Boards of Heywood, Heap and Hopwood were incorporated into a municipal borough in 1881, taking the name of Heywood.

MIDDLETON, *The Parish Church 1955* M311007

St Leonard's dates back to at least 1183 and it was largely rebuilt in 1414 and 1524. Its wooden steeple was added in 1709 and it is a rare and distinctive feature. Dominating the town, the Grade I listed church is in a conservation area. We view it here from Jubilee Park, which opened on 6 July 1889. Its exedra (a columned seating recess) and fountain were designed by Edgar Wood.

MIDDLETON AND HEYWOOD

MIDDLETON
Market Place 1955 M311001

Middleton was granted a market charter on 23 June 1791 and the market remained here until 1939. Surrounded by shops and inns, the Market Place was the hub of the town for many years. Ornamental gardens were laid out on the old Market Ground in 1948. They were much appreciated until 1972, when a roundabout replaced them at the time of the building of the Arndale Centre. The Assheton Arms, an old coaching inn, is at the bottom of Long Street, with the Williams Deacons and Salford Bank, designed by Edgar Wood, to its right.

MIDDLETON, *Ye Olde Boar's Head c1955* M311002

One of Middleton's oldest links with the past, this pub stands on the old great highway from Manchester to Yorkshire (now Long Street). A stone lintel in the cellar is dated 1632. The inn is thought to have formerly been part of a row of old cottages. A licensee was recorded as early as 1737.

FRANCIS FRITH'S - ROCHDALE

MIDDLETON
The Town Hall
c1955 M311004

Parkfield House became Middleton's second Town Hall in 1925. It was originally built for Daniel Burton, a bleacher of Rhodes; it passed to Salis Schwabe, who bought the bleach works and built the famous Rhodes Chimney. Parkfield House was demolished in 1978.

MIDDLETON, *Alkrington Hall c1955* M311005

This Georgian mansion, built in 1736 by Giacomo Leoni, the architect of Lyme Hall, Cheshire, has commanding views across the River Irk to Heaton Hall. When it was built for the Ashton Lever family it replaced an earlier hall built by Sir Darcy Lever and it was surrounded by a 700-acre estate. The Alkrington Garden Village now covers much of its former farmland.

MIDDLETON AND HEYWOOD

▲ **MIDDLETON**
The Central Gardens 1955 M311006

Opened in 1934 on the site of the former Middleton Hall corn mill, these gardens became another focal point for the town and a much-loved asset. They occupied the triangle at the junction of Manchester Old and New Roads. Visitors from the Manchester area spent time in them as part of a day out, often enjoying a snack at Redman's cafe on the left.

◀ *detail of M311006*

FRANCIS FRITH'S - ROCHDALE

MIDDLETON AND HEYWOOD

HEYWOOD
The Town Centre c1955
H228010

St Luke's Church was consecrated in October 1862 with seating for 1,000 and it dominates Heywood's centre. The Queen Anne Inn, to the right of Benefit Footwear (left), is much older, probably dating back to the reign of Queen Anne, as it appears on Heywood Hall Map of 1718. Petty Sessions were held here, along with hangings and cockfights at the rear. It has also served as a post office.

FRANCIS FRITH'S - ROCHDALE

▶ **HEYWOOD**
The Cenotaph c1955
H228009

The memorial to those who fell in the Great War was unveiled opposite St Luke's on 22 August 1925, and the Gardens of Remembrance opened the following year. The memorial depicts a figure of Peace, head bowed and holding the symbol of victory. The Carnegie Library on the left opened on 17 March 1906. Stanley Mill (right) was demolished for the building of Morrison's original supermarket.

MIDDLETON AND HEYWOOD

◀ **HEYWOOD**
The Rose Gardens, Queen's Park c1950
H228002

Queen's Park was opened on 2 August 1879 after Queen Victoria granted £11,000 from the estate of Charles Newhouse, a local wealthy cotton spinner who died intestate. The money purchased 20 acres of Heywood Hall's grounds for the park. A statue of Apollo stands in front of the gatehouse. The park is still very popular, with its attractive lawns sloping down towards the river Roach.

FRANCIS FRITH'S - ROCHDALE

HEYWOOD
The Fountain, Queen's Park c1955
H228003

The fountain is one of the park's most elegant features. Heritage lottery funding will soon provide £900,000 to upgrade the park, with its cafe, lawns, bandstand and lake.

HEYWOOD, *The Swans, Queen's Park c1955* H228005
Heywood Hall can just be seen in the background. It was the home of the de Heywood family and this house came into the possession of Heywood Corporation in 1927. They demolished it in 1956.

MIDDLETON AND HEYWOOD

HEYWOOD
Queen's Park c1950
H228006

A feature of the park is the unusually shaped white stone ornamentation. This small lake has been drained for many years, but a much larger lake is still one of the park's most important features. Alderman David Healey gave an additional 22 acres of land to the Corporation in 1923, part of it be used to build a bridge over the Roach by the park.

HEYWOOD, *Queen's Park Bridge c1955* H228007

It was 1931 before work started on Queen's Park Road. It was used as a project for locally unemployed men during the Depression and the bridge over the Roach was opened on 20 May 1933. St Luke's Church can be seen on the right.

BAMFORD, *The Village c1955* B358009

War Office Road joins Norden Road here. The manor of Bamford was owned by the de Bamford family from the 13th century until 1816, when it was sold to Joseph Fenton of Crimble. Some say the area known as War Office received its name during the Civil War, when Cromwell paid off 1,200 troops who had been held in reserve.

SIMPSON CLOUGH 1895 36776

Cheesden Brook passes under Ashworth Road, flowing to the right to join Naden Brook as it leaves Carr, Gelder and Bamford Woods. The brooks then powered a fulling mill, which Barker Bros extended for bleaching, dyeing and finishing. Wagons, with three carthorses each, took the finished cloth to Manchester warehouses, the first leaving at 6am and the last returning at 11pm every working day. James R Crompton Ltd, a specialist papermaking firm, bought the mill in around 1945 and they are still in business today. On the other side of Bury Road the brook powered another mill before joining the Roach.

ASHWORTH VALLEY 1895 36775
Ashworth is 3 miles from Rochdale and Bury and 1 mile from Heywood centre. Ashworth was formerly a detached part of Middleton. Its 100 acres of trees are recorded on an ancient woodland inventory and it is still an area of natural beauty. Ashworth Hall, with its own well remains, along with other buildings in Ashworth Fold close by has listed building status.

MIDDLETON AND HEYWOOD

CARR WOOD WATERFALL
1895 36771

The Ashworth Estate, covering 1,000 acres mainly of pasture, is still largely intact. This waterfall just south of School Lane had a race feeding the waterwheel of Ashworth Fulling Mill, which was to the right. The Ashworth family ran the mill in the early 1800s, along with Lower Clough Mill. They lived at Upper Clough Farm, which dates back to 1636. The family are buried at Ashworth Chapel.

CARR WOOD *1895* 36773

Just downstream of Carr Wood waterfall is this smaller weir, whose race carried water via a flagstone channel under fields to the left to the Ashworth Estate corn mill. Later the race served a bone mill and a small woollen and cotton mill nearby. To one sender of this postcard, it was 'not a bad view for this area'.

WHITWORTH AND HEALEY DELL

Whitworth used to be part of the Spotland Township of Rochdale. Its Local Board was set up in 1874 and it became a UDC in 1894, joining the newly created Rossendale Borough Council in 1974. Many of its farms were built in the 17th century, when sheep farming and handloom weaving predominated. The turnpike road built in the 1820s and the railway fifty years later improved access to both Lancashire and Yorkshire, giving impetus to industrial expansion. By 1870 there were 21 mills between Healey and Shawforth engaged in the fulling, dyeing, bleaching and manufacture of woollen and cotton goods. There were also boiler and shuttle making works, and stone quarries at Brittania and Facit. The latter became famous for Haslingden flag rock, used extensively in Lancashire for flagstone walls. Their stone provided paving in Trafalgar Square and Parliament Square and was used in the foundations of the Eiffel Tower. Quarry waste was used in the construction of the M62 motorway. Whitworth's last links with the textile trade were severed in 1993, when Mycock Ltd closed Spring Mill Works, Wallbank. The Whitworth Valley breaks out into spectacular scenery at Healey Dell, which has long been a jewel in its crown.

WHITWORTH, *St Bartholomew's Church 1951* W413009

James Taylor JP, one of the famous Whitworth Doctors, the bone setters, whose patients, including the Archbishop of Canterbury, came from far and wide, laid the cornerstone in 1847, on the site of a chapel of 1529. The London architect wanted to use Yorkshire pierpoints, but with so much local stone available he was outvoted. The congregation were not pleased either when stone from the last chapel was used for building the Whitworth Arms. Whitworth became a parish in 1866 following the Rochdale Vicarage Act. Dry rot and a fire threatened the future of St Bartholomew's in the early 1980s. It reopened in June 1987 - it is now shorter and lower than the building we see here.

WHITWORTH AND HEALEY DELL

WHITWORTH
From Sunny Bank 1951 W413012

The lane to Cock Hall is in the foreground and Whitworth High School playing fields now occupy the large field, with the school having been built to the right. Whitworth town centre is behind, with Market Street on the right.

WHITWORTH, *From the East c1955* W413006

Mills can be seen in the valley on the left, but the rural beauty of Whitworth is evident in this scene which was taken from Hopwood Barn Farm, sometimes known as Upwood Barn. Jim Mudd was the last occupant of the farm, which used to supply milk to Facit Mill.

FRANCIS FRITH'S - ROCHDALE

▶ **WHITWORTH AND FACIT** *1951* W413008

This photograph was taken from High Barn Farm. Dura Mill is nearest to the centre of the photograph with St Anselm's to the right. Tonge End Farm is behind the church. As in Shaw, the mills and the stone terraced houses, built for their operatives, dominate the valley.

WHITWORTH AND HEALEY DELL

◄ **WHITWORTH**
The Memorial Park
1951 W413014

The cenotaph can be seen to the left of centre of the park, which is on Market Street. The memorial is dedicated to Whitworth men who died in the two World Wars. On the extreme left is Facit Methodist chapel, which has since been demolished.

FRANCIS FRITH'S - ROCHDALE

▶ **WHITWORTH**
Facit 1951 W413002

This view looks north from above the Memorial Park, with the huge Facit New Mill on the right. Built of Accrington brick, it replaced a mill demolished in 1904. Facit New Mill was a cotton mill employing 700 people in its heyday – it closed in the mid 1960s. To the left of Market Street, Thomas Houghton's cotton waste mill has the smaller Spodden Mill to its right-hand side.

WHITWORTH AND HEALEY DELL

◀ **WHITWORTH**
St Anselm's Roman Catholic Church c1950 W413001

We are looking south-west from the Memorial Park; John Street and St Anselm's Church and school are behind Market Street. Three air raid shelters are in the field in front of the church. Whitworth's mills and quarries attracted Irish immigrants, who had to walk to St John's Roman Catholic Chapel, Rochdale until the Rev John Millward opened a Whitworth Mission in 1860. He helped to build the church and presbytery to his own design, using local stone. A primitive urn containing human bones, maybe of a Druid priest or warrior, was found when the foundations were being prepared. The church opened in 1869.

▶ **WHITWORTH**
Cowm Reservoir 1951
W413013

Rochdale Corporation started planning this reservoir in 1866. The existing water supply failed in 1868, when old pumps and barrels were used. Unexpected fissures in the reservoir bed meant that the lake was not satisfactorily filled until 1886. 4,000 trout were placed in Cowm and Spring Mill reservoirs in 1887. Tyre burning polluted the reservoir in 1975 and it has not been used for drinking water since.

FRANCIS FRITH'S - ROCHDALE

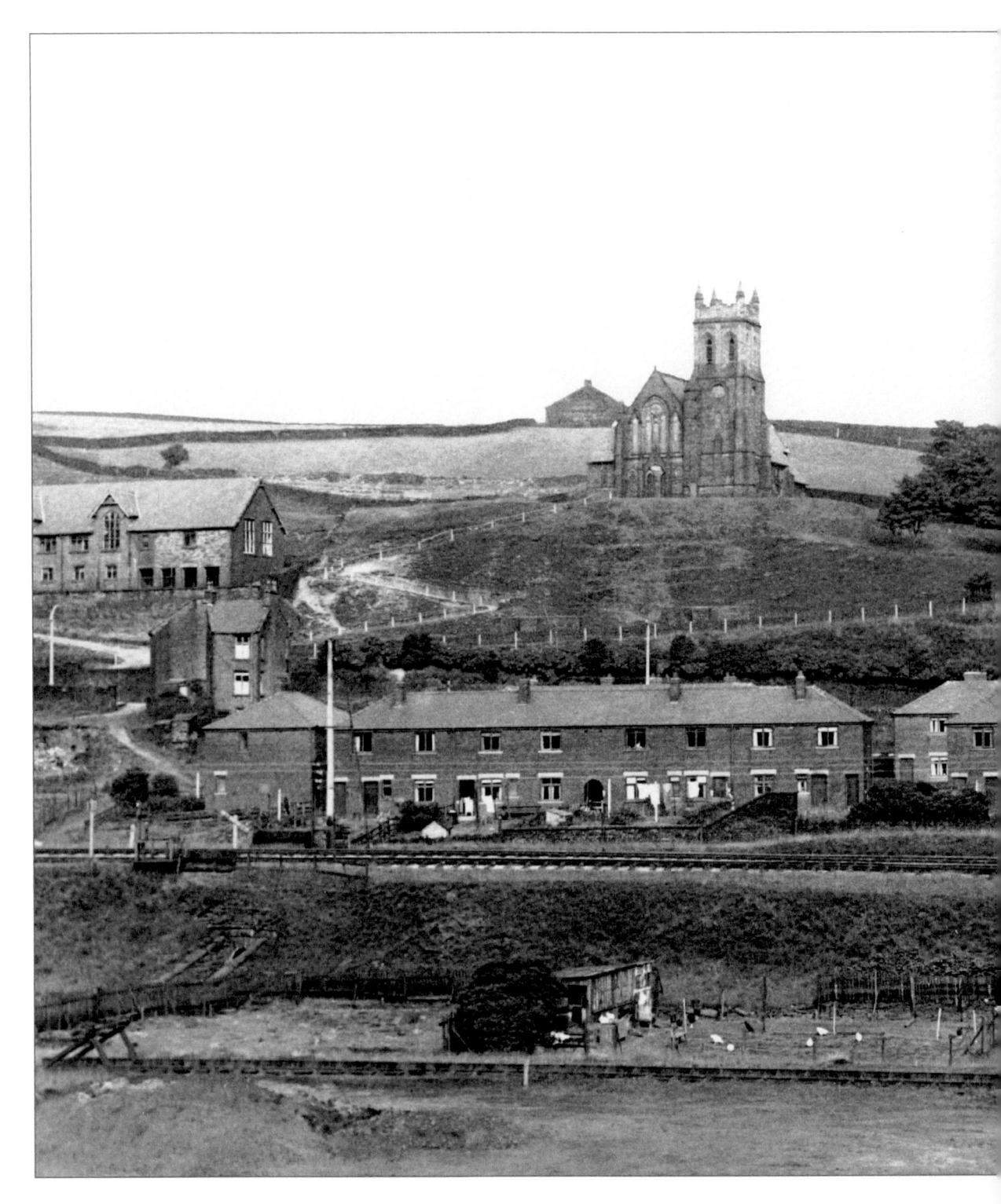

◀ **WHITWORTH**
Facit c1955
W413015

Facit, to the north of Whitworth, was elected for a church under the Rochdale Vicarage Act, 1866. St John's was consecrated on 1 December 1871. Seen here with its school on the left it commands excellent views over the railway, which was opened in 1870. All passenger trains ceased in 1947, but goods and special trains continued into the 1960s.

FRANCIS FRITH'S - ROCHDALE

HEALEY DELL VIADUCT *1895* 36767

This viaduct was constructed of local stone in 1867 for the Lancashire & Yorkshire Railway Company; the line opened in 1870 and closed in the 1960s. The viaduct is 105ft high, with its 8 arches each having a span of 30ft. The Spodden flows underneath with its mill stream, which formerly served 'Th' Owd Mill i' th' Thrutch'.

FRANCIS FRITH'S - ROCHDALE

HEALEY DELL *1913* 65607

The river Spodden flows south from Whitworth, cutting through Healey Dell, formerly Healey Thrutch. The word 'thrutch' is of Anglo Saxon origin, denoting an area where a river makes a deep cutting through rocks, with a corn mill often nearby, as in this case. Healey Dell cutting is 100ft deep, an indication of its age and little has changed since those ancient times.

HEALEY DELL, *The Fairies' Chapel 1913* 65608

The great flood of 4 July 1838 largely destroyed the 'chapel', which was a cavern in the rock with a 'pulpit', 'reading desk' and 'seats' carved out of the stone. The flood rose to 15ft at Spotland Bridge at the time. In his book 'Traditions of Lancashire', John Roby wrote about the chapel and of a lovely maiden whose love was unrequited: 'Maid, Wife and Widow in one day, this shall be thy destiny'. He also wrote of a miller who chased a white hare up the Thrutch. Other writers have linked the chapel with Robin Hood!

HEALEY DELL 1898 41031

Three-storey stone cottages on Market Street can just be seen at the top of this photograph. There is another man-made weir above the rocks in the Thrutch. Most of the dell is much more densely wooded today.

HEALEY DELL c1915 R42304

This shelter was opened in 1912 in the area known as the Spaw (a corruption of Spodden). There was a similar shelter near the Fairies' Chapel. The dell has always attracted walkers, such as groups of young people strolling through it after Sunday evening service at local chapels. It was also a popular venue for church outings and picnics.

FRANCIS FRITH'S - ROCHDALE

HEALEY DELL
1898 41030

The 188 acres of Healey Dell became a Nature Reserve in 1976. Oak, birch and beech trees predominate and there are over 400 species of flora and over 60 species of birds. The corn mill became a fulling mill in 1636 and remains of old stone fulling tanks can still be seen.

HEALEY DELL WATERFALL *1895* 36769
There are several waterfalls in the dell, most of them created by man-made weirs with races from them serving mills, some of which were linked with Healey Hall.

INDEX

Around Rochdale
    Castleton 52-53, 54-55, 56
    Falinge Park 50, 51, 52
    Hollingworth Lake 44, 45, 48-49, 50-51
    Littleborough 45, 46-47, 48-49, 50-51
    Shaw 58-59, 60-61
    St John's Roman Catholic Church 52
    Walsden 57, 59

Ashworth Valley 74

Bamford 72

Carr Wood 75

Healey Dell 84-85, 86, 87, 88

Heywood 66-67, 68-69, 70, 71

Middleton 62, 63, 64, 65

Rochdale
    Broadfield Park 14, 15, 16
    Broadway 33, 34-35
    Church Steps 12
    Drake Street 40-41, 43
    The Esplanade 16, 18-19, 20
    The Fountain 17
    The Friends' Meeting House 32
    Grammar School 24
    John Bright's Statue 31
    Manor House 25
    The Memorial 21
    Memorial Gardens 27
    Newgate 40
    Nurses' Home 24
    One Ash 32
    Parish Church 13, 14-15
    The Park Slopes 20-21
    Parker Sprout Gardens 13
    Post Office 27
    The Technical School 43
    Town Centre 36-37, 38-39, 40-41
    Town Hall 22-23
    Town Hall Square 30
    The War Memorial 26, 27
    Yorkshire Street 28-29, 42-43

Simpson Clough 73

Whitworth 76, 77, 78-79, 80-81, 82-83

FRITH PRODUCTS & SERVICES

Francis Frith would doubtless be pleased to know that the pioneering publishing venture he started in 1860 still continues today. Over a hundred and forty years later, The Francis Frith Collection continues in the same innovative tradition and is now one of the foremost publishers of vintage photographs in the world. Some of the current activities include:

INTERIOR DECORATION

Today Frith's photographs can be seen framed and as giant wall murals in thousands of pubs, restaurants, hotels, banks, retail stores and other public buildings throughout the country. In every case they enhance the unique local atmosphere of the places they depict and provide reminders of gentler days in an increasingly busy and frenetic world.

PRODUCT PROMOTIONS

Frith products are used by many major companies to promote the sales of their own products or to reinforce their own history and heritage. Frith promotions have been used by Hovis bread, Courage beers, Scots Porage Oats, Colman's mustard, Cadbury's foods, Mellow Birds coffee, Dunhill pipe tobacco, Guinness, and Bulmer's Cider.

GENEALOGY AND FAMILY HISTORY

As the interest in family history and roots grows world-wide, more and more people are turning to Frith's photographs of Great Britain for images of the towns, villages and streets where their ancestors lived; and, of course, photographs of the churches and chapels where their ancestors were christened, married and buried are an essential part of every genealogy tree and family album.

FRITH PRODUCTS

All Frith photographs are available Framed or just as Mounted Prints and Posters (size 23 x 16 inches). These may be ordered from the address below. Other products available are- Address Books, Calendars, Jigsaws, Canvas Prints, Notelets and local and prestige books.

THE INTERNET

Already ninety thousand Frith photographs can be viewed and purchased on the internet through the Frith websites and a myriad of partner sites.

For more detailed information on Frith companies and products, look at this site:
www.francisfrith.com

See the complete list of Frith Books at: www.francisfrith.com
This web site is regularly updated with the latest list of publications from The Francis Frith Collection. If you wish to buy books relating to another part of the country that your local bookshop does not stock, you may purchase on-line.

For further information, trade, or author enquiries please contact us at the address below:
The Francis Frith Collection, Unit 6, Oakley Business Park, Wylye Road, Dinton, Wiltshire SP3 5EU.
Tel: +44 (0)1722 716 376 Fax: +44 (0)1722 716 881 Email: sales@francisfrith.co.uk

See Frith products on the internet at www.francisfrith.com

FREE PRINT OF YOUR CHOICE

Mounted Print
Overall size 14 x 11 inches (355 x 280mm)

Choose any Frith photograph in this book.
Simply complete the Voucher opposite and return it with your remittance for £3.50 (to cover postage and handling) and we will print the photograph of your choice in SEPIA (size 11 x 8 inches) and supply it in a cream mount with a burgundy rule line (overall size 14 x 11 inches).
Please note: aerial photographs and photographs with a reference number starting with a "Z" are not Frith photographs and cannot be supplied under this offer. Offer valid for delivery to one UK address only.

PLUS: **Order additional Mounted Prints at HALF PRICE - £9.50 each** (normally £19.00)
If you would like to order more Frith prints from this book, possibly as gifts for friends and family, you can buy them at half price (with no additional postage and handling costs).

PLUS: **Have your Mounted Prints framed**
For an extra £18.00 per print you can have your mounted print(s) framed in an elegant polished wood and gilt moulding, overall size 16 x 13 inches (no additional postage and handling required).

IMPORTANT!

These special prices are only available if you use this form to order. You must use the ORIGINAL VOUCHER on this page (no copies permitted). We can only despatch to one UK address. This offer cannot be combined with any other offer.

Send completed Voucher form to:
The Francis Frith Collection, Unit 6, Oakley Business Park, Wylye Road, Dinton, Wiltshire SP3 5EU

CHOOSE A PHOTOGRAPH FROM THIS BOOK

Voucher for **FREE** and Reduced Price Frith Prints

Please do not photocopy this voucher. Only the original is valid, so please fill it in, cut it out and return it to us with your order.

Picture ref no	Page no	Qty	Mounted @ £9.50	Framed + £18.00	Total Cost £
		1	Free of charge*	£	£
			£9.50	£	£
			£9.50	£	£
			£9.50	£	£
			£9.50	£	£
			£9.50	£	£

Please allow 28 days for delivery. Offer available to one UK address only

* Post & handling   £3.50

Total Order Cost   £

Title of this book ....

I enclose a cheque/postal order for £ ....
made payable to 'The Francis Frith Collection'

OR please debit my Mastercard / Visa / Maestro card, details below

Card Number:

Issue No (Maestro only):   Valid from (Maestro):

Card Security Number: Expires:

Signature:

Name Mr/Mrs/Ms ....
Address ....
....
....
.... Postcode ....
Daytime Tel No ....
Email ....

Valid to 31/12/12

Free Print – see overleaf

Can you help us with information about any of the Frith photographs in this book?

We are gradually compiling an historical record for each of the photographs in the Frith archive. It is always fascinating to find out the names of the people shown in the pictures, as well as insights into the shops, buildings and other features depicted.

If you recognize anyone in the photographs in this book, or if you have information not already included in the author's caption, do let us know. We would love to hear from you, and will try to publish it in future books or articles.

An Invitation from The Francis Frith Collection to Share Your Memories

The 'Share Your Memories' feature of our website allows members of the public to add personal memories relating to the places featured in our photographs, or comment on others already added. Seeing a place from your past can rekindle forgotten or long held memories. Why not visit the website, find photographs of places you know well and add YOUR story for others to read and enjoy? We would love to hear from you!

www.francisfrith.com/memories

Our production team

Frith books are produced by a small dedicated team at offices near Salisbury. Most have worked with the Frith Collection for many years. All have in common one quality: they have a passion for the Frith Collection.

Frith Books and Gifts

We have a wide range of books and gifts available on our website utilising our photographic archive, many of which can be individually personalised.

www.francisfrith.com